2/10

Safety at Home

By MaryLee Knowlton
Photography by Gregg Andersen

Crabtree Publishing Company

www.crabtreebooks.com

Crabtree Publishing Company

www.crabtreebooks.com

3 1561 00232 4766

Author: MaryLee Knowlton
Project coordinator: Robert Walker
Editor: Reagan Miller
Proofreaders: Molly Aloian, Crystal Sikkens
Production coordinator: Katherine Kantor
Prepress technicians: Samara Parent, Ken Wright
Design: Westgraphix/Tammy West

Written, developed, and produced by
Water Buffalo Books/Mark Sachner Publishing Services

Photographs: © Gregg Andersen/Gallery 19

Acknowledgments:
The publisher, producer, and photographer
gratefully acknowledge the following people for their
participation in the making of this book:
In Soldotna, Alaska: Dallas Armstrong, Mary Armstrong,
Chris Kempf, Er Kempf, Jackie Kempf, Etta Mae Near,
Jerome Near, Janet O'Toole, Mike O'Toole, John Pothast.
In Mankato, Minnesota: Debbie Benke, Candee Deichman,
Liz Goertzen, Syndie Johnson, Brianna Ostoff. And a special
thanks is offered to the dozens of school children, staff, and
parents who gave generously and enthusiastically of their
time and talent in the making of this book.

Library and Archives Canada Cataloguing in Publication

Knowlton, MaryLee, 1946-
     Safety at home / MaryLee Knowlton ; photography by
Gregg Andersen.

(Staying safe)
Includes index.
ISBN 978-0-7787-4316-3 (bound).--ISBN 978-0-7787-4321-7 (pbk.)

     1. Home accidents--Prevention--Juvenile literature. 2. Safety
education--Juvenile literature. I. Andersen, Gregg II. Title.
III. Series: Staying safe (St. Catharines, Ont.)

Library of Congress Cataloging-in-Publication Data

Knowlton, MaryLee, 1946-
    Safety at home / by MaryLee Knowlton ; photography by Gregg Andersen.
       p. cm. -- (Staying safe)
    Includes index.
    ISBN-13: 978-0-7787-4321-7 (pbk. : alk. paper)
    ISBN-10: 0-7787-4321-7 (pbk. : alk. paper)
    ISBN-13: 978-0-7787-4316-3 (reinforced library binding : alk. paper)
    ISBN-10: 0-7787-4316-0 (reinforced library binding : alk. paper)
    1. Home accidents--Prevention--Juvenile literature. 2. Children's accidents--Prevention--Juvenile
literature. 3. Safety education--Juvenile literature. I. Title. II. Series.

HV675.5.K67 2009
613.6--dc22

                                                   2008036589

Published in Canada
Crabtree Publishing
616 Welland Ave.
St. Catharines, ON
L2M 5V6

Published in the United States
Crabtree Publishing
PMB16A
350 Fifth Ave., Suite 3308
New York, NY 10118

Published in the United Kingdom
Crabtree Publishing
White Cross Mills
High Town, Lancaster
LA1 4XS

Published in Australia
Crabtree Publishing
386 Mt. Alexander Rd.
Ascot Vale (Melbourne)
VIC 3032

Contents

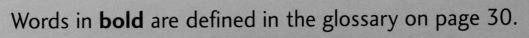

Words in **bold** are defined in the glossary on page 30.

Staying Safe at Home

Your family has done what they can to make your home a safe and **comfortable** place. Some safety decisions are up to you, however. How can you make choices that will keep you and your family safe at home?

In this book, each section presents a home safety **hazard** or problem.

Here is how the book works:

First, you will read about a home safety problem.

Second, you will choose how to solve the problem.

Third, you will learn about the **consequence**,
or outcome, of each choice.

For every bad
consequence,
you will see a "no" sign.

For every good
consequence, you
will see a gold star.

Finally, you will learn which is the best choice
and why.

You will also learn about ways to stay safe in your
own house and yard. Telling your friends what you
learn will help them make safe choices, too.

Stair Safety

Playing on the stairs can be fun. You can turn them into a bus, or a train, or even an airplane. It is important to play safely. There should be no running or pushing.

What else should you do to make the stairs safe for everyone?

What's happening?

You've been playing on the stairs with your toys and now you want to go outside. What should you do with your toys?

What should you do?

A. Leave the toys on the stairs and jump over them carefully on your way outside.

B. Try to clear a path by pushing your toys over to the side of the stairs.

C. Pick up the toys and put them away before you go outside.

Which is the best choice?

Turn the page........... and find out!

What happens next:

If you choose A . . .

You might miss a step and fall down the stairs.

If you choose B . . .

Your mom or dad might trip on the toys and fall down the stairs!

You make the stairs safe
for yourself and for others.

The best choice is C.
Pick up your toys as soon as you are finished
playing. Be sure to put the toys back where
they belong.

What have you learned?

Picking up your toys is the only way
to be sure that you keep the
stairs safe for everyone.

Using Hot Water Safely

It's important to stay clean, and taking a shower or a bath is the best way to keep your entire body clean. The hardest thing about taking a shower or a bath is figuring out how to make the water just the right **temperature**.

How can you get clean without making the water too hot or too cold?

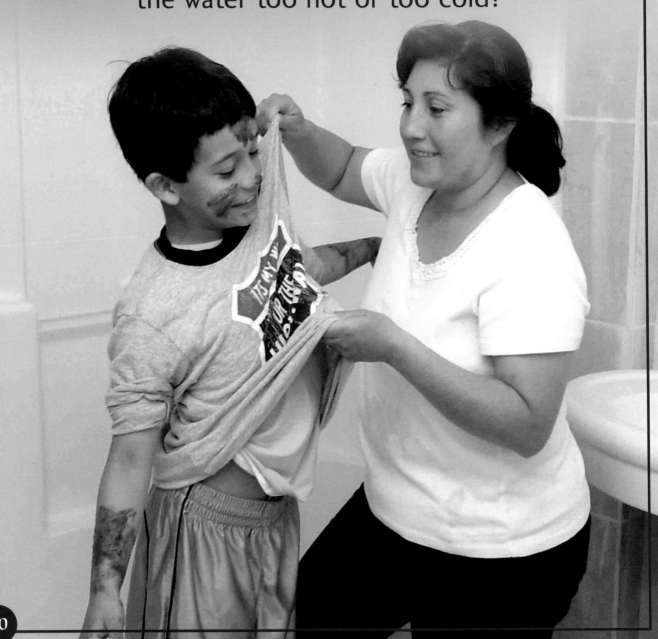

What's happening?

You are covered with dirt after playing in a muddy field, and your mom thinks you need a shower.

What should you do?

A. Get in the shower, turn on just the cold water, and then **adjust** the hot water until the water reaches the right temperature.

B. Get in the shower and turn on both the hot and cold water full blast.

C. Before you get in the shower, let the water run for a few minutes. Test the water by letting it run quickly over your hand and wrist. When it feels comfortable, get in the shower!

Which is the best choice?

Turn the page and find out!

What happens next:

If you choose A . . .

You could get very cold as you wait for the water to warm up.

If you choose B . . .

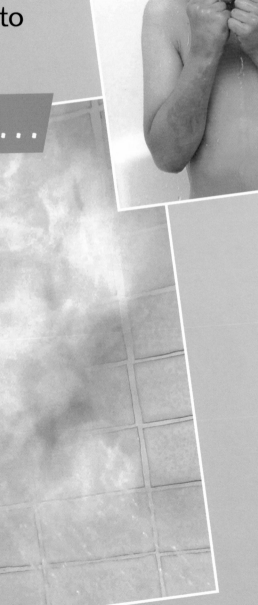

The water may be too hot and you could be badly burned.

The water is just right.
You scrub off the dirt and come
out of the shower clean and refreshed!

The best choice is C.

Be sure the water is the right temperature before you get in. If you're not sure what to do, ask a grownup in charge.

What have you learned?

The water you use in your home can be hot enough to burn you badly. Always be sure you know how hot or how cold the water is before you get into a shower or a bathtub.

Safety in the Kitchen

It is not safe for you to handle sharp knives or use the stove. There may be some foods you can prepare by yourself, however, if a grownup tells you it is safe.

What else do you need to think about to keep safe in the kitchen?

What's happening?

You want to make yourself a peanut butter sandwich. The peanut butter is on a high shelf, however. It's too high for you to reach from the floor. What should you do?

What should you do?

A. Use a chair to climb up on the counter to reach the peanut butter.

B. Find something long, like a spoon, to push the jar close to the edge of the shelf so you can catch it as it falls.

C. Ask a grownup to get the peanut butter down for you.

Which is the best choice?

Turn the page.............
and find out!

What happens next:

If you choose A . . .

The chair might tip over. You could fall, or you might not be able to climb down safely! 🚫

If you choose B . . .

The jar might fall too fast for you to catch it. It could hit you on the head or smash onto the floor. You could be hurt—or get in trouble! 🚫

You have what you need for your sandwich. You're not hurt, and you're not in trouble!

The best choice is C.
You can also ask to have the things you need put on a lower shelf.

What have you learned?

Never try to get something that is over your head. Always ask a grownup to get it down for you.

Keep Germs in Their Place!

Even if you eat healthy snacks, **germs** can get onto the food and into your body.

How can you avoid getting sick from letting germs get into your body from the food you eat?

What's happening?

You have been throwing a stick for your dog and teaching him to fetch. Now you're hungry. There's a bowl of apples on the counter.

What should you do?

A. Grab an apple and gobble it down.

B. Wash your hands with soap and warm water, and then gobble down the apple.

C. Wash your hands with soap and warm water. Then wash the apple under cold running water. Be sure to dry your hands when you're done. Now it's time to eat!

Which is the best choice?

Turn the page............ and find out!

What happens next:

If you choose A . . .

Your hands have been touching many things, even the stick that was inside your dog's mouth! Yuck! The germs on your hands get on the foods you touch. When you eat these foods, the germs end up inside your body. They can make you sick. 🚫

If you choose B . . .

It is important we wash our hands with soap and water, but we also need to wash fruits and vegetables under cold running water. The outside of the apple may have **chemicals** on it that helped it grow or kept insects off. This stuff may not taste good, and it's not good for you! 🚫

You and your food are free from dirt and germs that do not belong in your body. The only thing that goes into your body is food!

The best choice is C.

Wash your hands and your fruit before you eat.

what have you learned?

Germs, dirt, and chemicals do not belong in your body. Always wash your hands with soap and warm water before you eat anything. Also wash fruit and vegetables under cold running water.

Gross GarBage!

Germs can grow on food wrappers and dirty dishes. The garbage we leave when we're done eating can also attract insects and animals!

What can you do to keep your home safe from germs and **pests**?

What's happening?

You've been hanging out in your room watching TV and eating snacks. Juice boxes, banana peels, and granola bar wrappers are all over the place. What should you do about them?

What should you do?

A. Hide them under your bed.

B. Leave them there for your big sister to clean up.

C. Gather up the trash and dirty dishes. Put all the cans, cardboard, and plastic in the recycling bin. All the other trash belongs in the containers your family uses for garbage.

Which is the best choice?

Turn the page........▸ and find out!

What happens next:

If you choose A . . .

Garbage is food for germs, insects, and even rats! You don't want to share your bedroom with these critters! 🚫

If you choose B . . .

Your big sister might not see everything, and you still might be sharing your room with bugs and animals. Even if she picks up all the garbage, she's not going to be very happy with you! 🚫

The garbage and dirty dishes end up
in the kitchen where they belong. ⭐

The best choice is C.

Your room smells good and stays clean. You show
your mom that you can keep it that way, so she
lets you have snacks in your room!

What have you learned?

Garbage is food for germs and animal pests.
Always clean up after yourself so your room is a safe
place for sleeping and playing. You don't want it to
look or smell like a garbage can!

Play It Safe!

It's fun to go out and play with your friends, but you have to stay safe when you are playing outside, too. Make sure you choose a safe place to play, and stay away from traffic in the street!

How can you be sure you are safe when there are cars around?

What's happening?

You and your friend Sara are playing catch on the sidewalk when the ball bounces into the street.

What should you do?

A. Chase after the ball before it rolls to the other side of the street.

B. Ask Sara to go and get the ball.

C. Ask a parent or another adult watching you to return the ball to you.

Which is the best choice?

Turn the page and find out!

What happens next:

If you choose A . . .

You could get hit by a car while chasing after your ball. 🚫

If you choose B . . .

Sara could get hit by a car while chasing after the ball. 🚫

An adult returns your ball. Everyone is safe, and you can continue playing. Also, you show other kids that you know not to run into the street.

The best choice is C.

People driving cars don't expect kids to run into the street. A car is big and needs room to stop. You don't want to be in its way! Always ask a grownup to help you get anything that has gone out into the street.

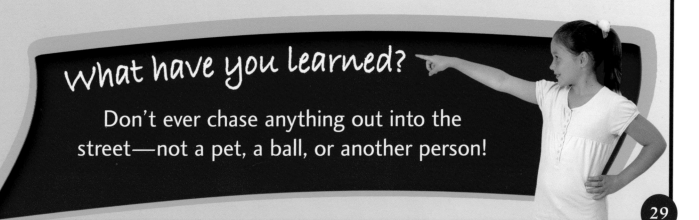

What have you learned?

Don't ever chase anything out into the street—not a pet, a ball, or another person!

Glossary

adjust To move the different parts of a machine or an object so that they fit or work well together

chemicals Substances produced by humans or in nature that have an effect on other things. Chemicals can be used to help plants grow and keep insects off

comfortable Feeling relaxed, safe, or at home

consequence The result or effect of an action; a thing that happens as a result of something else happening

containers Things that are used to store, or keep, other things in

fetch To go after something and bring it back

germs Living things that are too tiny to see but that can live on food and garbage and make you sick

hazard A danger or a chance to get hurt

pests Animals or insects, such as mice, rats, or cockroaches, that can carry disease and be harmful to plants, humans, and other animals

temperature How hot or cold something is, measured in numbers called degrees

BOOKS

Stop Drop and Roll (A Book about Fire Safety). Margery Cuyler. Simon & Schuster Children's Publishing, 2001.

Home Safety (Living Well). Lucia Raatma. Child's World, 2003.

Traffic and Safety (Start-Up Geography). Anna Lee. Evans Brothers, 2003.

Safety Around the House (Tough Topics). Ana Deboo. Heinemann, 2007.

WEBSITES

Code Red Rover
http://coderedrover.org
Kids can read and listen as Red Rover and his friends introduce them to great activities that teach and illustrate safety at home.

Kids.gov: The Official Kids' Portal for the U.S. Government
http://www.kids.gov/k_5/k_5_health_safety.shtml
This site provides information and activities that teach and encourage safety. It also includes an amazing list of links to other sites about safety—including bicycle safety, food safety, stranger safety, and safety around animals.

Index

Printed in the U.S.A.